essential careers™

A Career as a Heavy Equipment Operator

Henrietta Toth

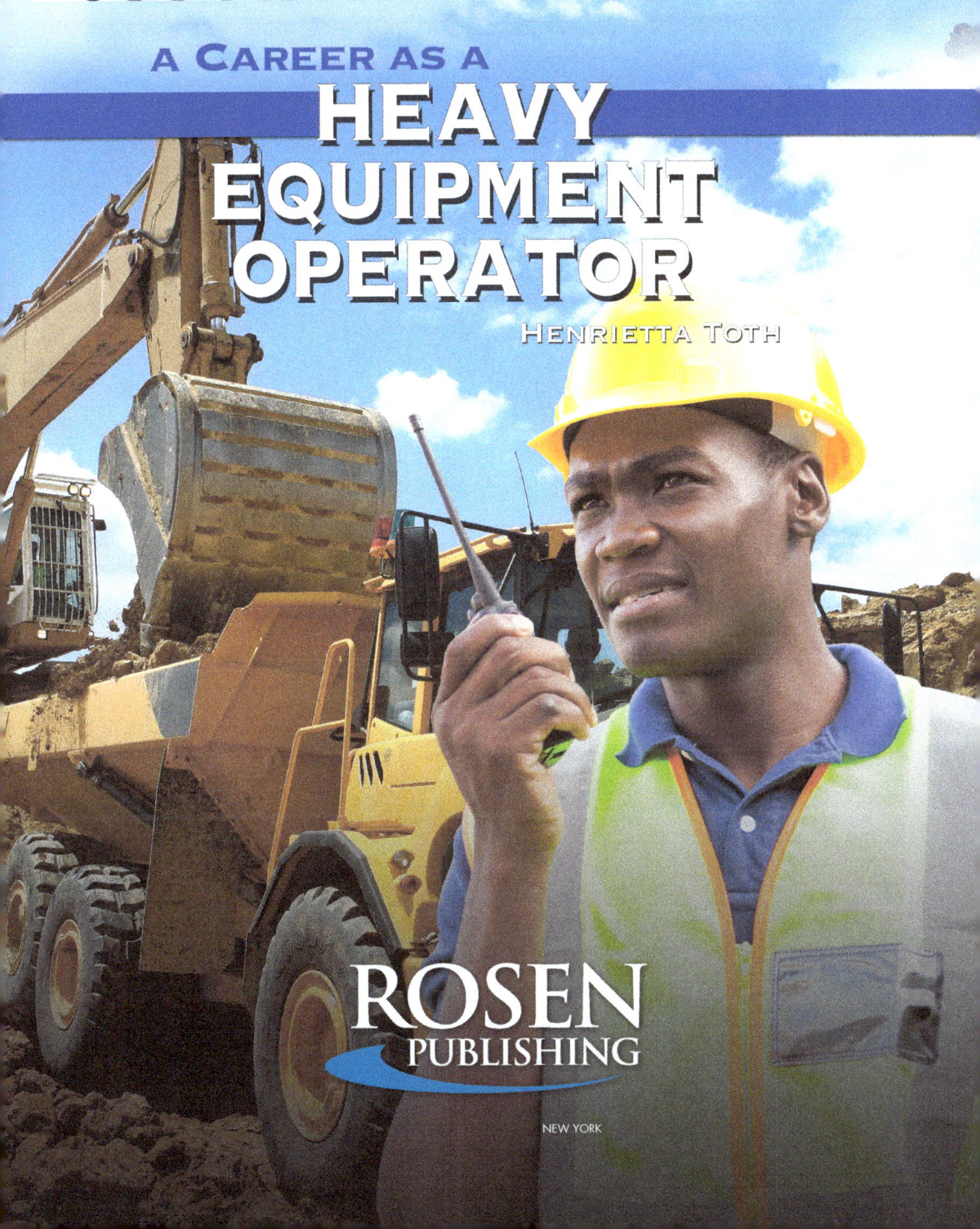

ROSEN PUBLISHING

NEW YORK

For my niece Emi, who likes to build and create things

Published in 2016 by The Rosen Publishing Group, Inc.
29 East 21st Street, New York, NY 10010

First Edition

Library of Congress Cataloging-in-Publication Data

Toth, Henrietta, author.
A career as a heavy equipment operator / Henrietta Toth. -- First edition.
pages cm. -- (Essential careers)
Includes bibliographical references and index.
ISBN 978-1-4994-6215-9 (library bound)
1. Construction industry--Vocational guidance--Juvenile literature. 2. Construction equipment operators--Juvenile literature. 3. Construction equipment--Juvenile literature. I. Title. II. Series: Essential careers.
TH159.T68 2016
690'.023--dc23

2015024389

Manufactured in the United States of America

contents

INTRO

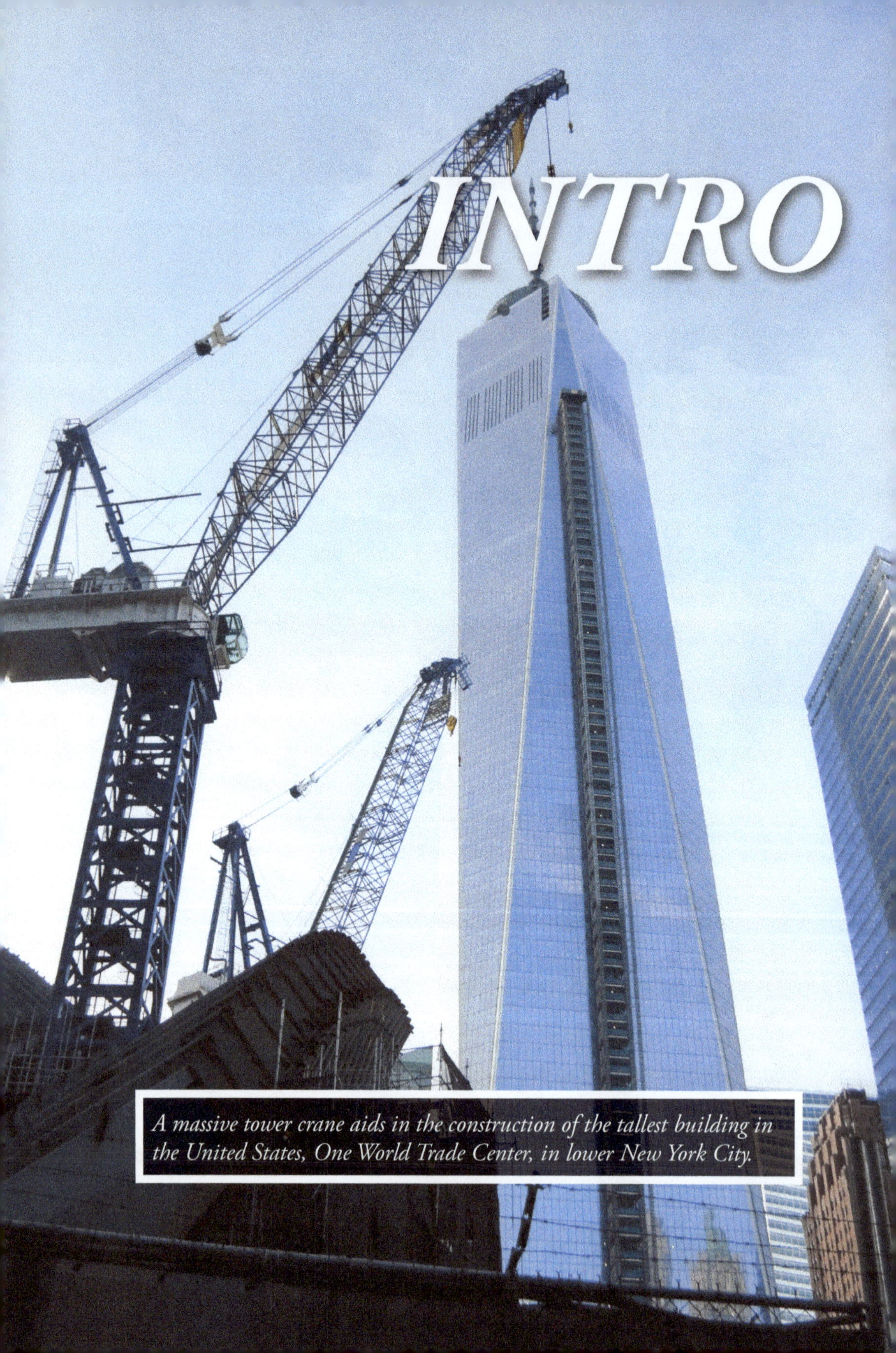

A massive tower crane aids in the construction of the tallest building in the United States, One World Trade Center, in lower New York City.

DUCTION

As workers were lifting the steel spire into place on top of One World Trade Center, they got a spectacular bird's-eye view of New York City and New Jersey. Using a massive tower crane, the spire was hoisted section by section more than 1,300 feet (400 meters) above the streets of Manhattan. Mobilizing such heavy equipment on the tallest building in the United States required dedicated skills and agility at high altitudes and in windy conditions. America's best-known construction site also had its share of safety risks as hundreds of workers moved large loads of concrete and steel 104 stories into the sky.

Operators of heavy equipment have the opportunity to work on projects of a grand scale, such as One World Trade Center, and also at smaller building sites, with both making important contributions to the community. The term "heavy equipment" describes any large, powerful, multiton machine—such as excavators and tower cranes—that are used in construction and engineering projects. Heavy equipment operators drive and control this machinery that changes a landscape by moving earth or raising the frame of a building.

Heavy equipment operators are always busy on small and large projects from coast to coast, and job opportunities can even be found overseas. The construction and repair of roads, bridges, buildings, railroads, and subways require the use of specialized heavy-duty equipment operated by skilled men and women. Other fields of work using heavy machinery include mining, forestry, agriculture, shipbuilding, and even the military. Each line of work has specific positions and skill requirements and offers different levels of advancement.

A career as a heavy equipment operator can be exciting and rewarding, especially when working to finish a project. Seeing that new road, rail, or building offers a sense of accomplishment. An aptitude for and interest in developing the necessary skills needed to operate heavy equipment is essential. Flexibility, creativity, attention to details, teamwork, and willingness to learn to use new machinery are just some of the requirements for developing a successful career as an operator. The ability to handle duties that vary from day to day and in all kinds of environments is also an important part of the job. The path to a career as a heavy equipment operator is varied and can include college courses, apprenticeships, certificate programs, and on-the-job training. Learning about the field of heavy equipment operation while in middle school or high school can help pave the way toward landing a job in a line of work that offers personal satisfaction and financial security.

In a changing economy, finding any job can be a difficult task. For heavy equipment operators, the search for employment is made easier because heavy vehicles are always needed for all types of building, repair, and demolition jobs. Thus, heavy equipment operators can look forward to an enduring and dependable occupation. Women and minorities as well are finding that this field can be a good career choice, making for a diverse workforce. In addition, the possibilities for even greater challenges exist as new technology drives heavy equipment operation forward into the twenty-first century.

chapter 1

WHAT'S THE JOB ABOUT?

Almost every child's toy collection at one time or another consists of a dump truck or some similar miniature construction vehicle. Many boys and girls have pretended to be the operators of excavators as they scooped up sand or dirt and deposited it elsewhere. In the adult world, operating heavy equipment is a career option that offers creativity, challenges, and rewards.

Exploring career paths in the field of heavy equipment operation can seem intimidating. What exactly does a heavy equipment operator do? How do those massive machines really work? Finding out whether a career will be a good fit takes some homework, but answering all the questions this raises can also be enjoyable and profitable in the long run.

THE ROLE OF AN OPERATOR

Who hasn't been stuck in traffic while the operator of an asphalt spreader moves the vehicle over a section of road? The operator of such a large piece of equipment has a key job in building or repairing a road that is used by hundreds or even thousands of drivers a day. It is an indispensable job with real responsibility and one that provides a vital service to the community.

The primary role of a heavy equipment operator is to use any type of large or towering machine with great skill and ease. Operators must be comfortable with the mechanical power

A team of heavy equipment operators uses pneumatic steam road rollers to pack down fresh asphalt while constructing a highway.

these machines exert as they follow through on instructions for a project. The several moving parts of a piece of heavy equipment have specific functions that together achieve a certain task. Therefore, the smooth operation of any machinery depends on the technical expertise of the operator.

An especially important duty of a heavy equipment operator is exercising strong safety skills. This includes watching out for other members of the work crew, as well as taking into consideration members of the public who might need to navigate through or around a work zone. Working with costly and possibly dangerous equipment means that an operator needs to be constantly watchful in order to spot and avoid a hazardous situation.

A Career in Demand

As long as there are roads to build, earth to move, and structures to erect, there will be a need for heavy equipment operators. Job opportunities can range from repairing existing roads to working on massive multimillion-dollar projects, such as the New NY Bridge in Tarrytown, New York, one of the largest bridge and highway construction projects in North America. Replacing older and outdated structures—such as the Edmonton Arena in Alberta, Canada—increases the demand for operators.

The expansion of building in certain sectors and the need for replacement in others means that operators of heavy machinery will always be needed in the labor force. Any shortage of qualified operators can slow or delay the progress of construction projects. Highly trained operators are most sought after by employers. With their specialized skills in running and maintaining various heavy machines, these operators play important roles in any job assignments they take.

Areas of Work

The most obvious course of work for heavy equipment operators is in building construction. Whether building houses or skyscrapers, operators are there to push, pull, move, dig, and raise all manner of loads. Residential and commercial construction provides the majority of job openings for operators. State and local road and highway departments are another clear choice. Particularly interesting options include building a resort, theme park, museum, or airport runway.

HISTORY AND DEVELOPMENT OF HEAVY EQUIPMENT OPERATION

Seeing the modern heavy equipment used at today's construction sites makes it hard to imagine that the ancient Egyptians used a type of heavy equipment, a primitive crane, four thousand years ago to build the pyramids.

Some three thousand years ago, the Greeks relied on cranes to construct temples and theaters of heavy stone, many of which exist today. The ancient Romans used some forms of large machinery about two thousand years ago. Hoists, pulleys, and an early type of crane made it possible to erect the aqueducts that carried water throughout the Roman Empire. By the Middle Ages, the crane had evolved to aid in the design and construction of cavernous cathedrals.

Concrete is poured into the foundation of Hoover Dam on the Colorado River, a remarkable construction project of the 1930s.

Of course, for centuries humans and animals pulled the hefty equipment needed to build roads, bridges, and buildings. The increasing use of steam- and gasoline-powered engines in the nineteenth century brought about rapid development in heavy machinery. By the twentieth century, these new methods of powering equipment made possible massive building feats such as the Hoover Dam and the Panama Canal. Bulldozers appeared on the construction scene in the 1930s. These modern earth-moving machines emerged from the designs of Robert Gilmour LeTourneau. From the 1920s through the 1940s, LeTourneau developed several kinds of large equipment that could transport earth more speedily and efficiently. In the twenty-first century, advanced technology—such as computerized systems that guide operators—continues to bring even greater advances in the operation of heavy equipment.

Oil and gas fields offer lucrative work, as do mining and timber operations. Utility companies need heavy equipment workers to provide and maintain essential services such as electricity, water, and sewage systems. Shipping ports employ operators of heavy machinery to offload cargo vessels. Also, all branches of the military have operators in their ranks.

Other employers of heavy equipment include commercial landscapers who refashion large areas of land, most often around office complexes and multiunit housing compounds. Structural moving—as in moving a building—also uses heavy machinery to relocate an endangered or historic house, church, or barn. Modern agriculture relies on small and large tractors.

SPECIFIC JOBS

Heavy equipment operators work with different types of machinery geared toward the needs of a particular job. Bulldozer operators excavate and load earth or other materials. Building a road requires the services of road grader operators, tamping machine operators, asphalt spreader operators, and concrete paving machine operators.

Forklift, backhoe, and tractor operators carry out numerous functions on small and large projects. More specialized

Cranes tower over a China Shipping cargo ship in the port of Oakland in San Francisco Bay, ready to assist in the loading and offloading of containers.

equipment is used by tower crane operators, who need to reach certain heights, and pile driver operators, who pound piles of concrete or steel into the ground for foundations.

Although many operators prefer working on one machine over another, they are often trained in the use of several pieces of equipment. This broad knowledge and set of skills helps to make these operators more employable as the requirements change from one project to the next.

A TYPICAL DAY

For heavy equipment operators, the day can begin early, late, or on the weekend, depending on the job. Getting to work ahead of the scheduled start time gives operators a chance to check the equipment they will be using and the site assigned to them. An average day might include demolition work or shifting tons of soil to another location. The schedule on any given day goes according to the functions that will move the job along.

Sometimes operators come across an unusual and rare find. For example, a woman manning heavy equipment in Alberta, Canada, unearthed the fossil of an ancient marine reptile. It's one of several fossils found while mining oil in Alberta. Another exciting find occurred in the southern Chinese city of Heyuan. Workers doing road repairs dug up forty-three fossilized dinosaur eggs measuring 5 inches (13 centimeters) in diameter that are estimated to be eighty-nine million years old.

Construction sites sometimes yield archaeological discoveries, such as this tooth and skull of a more than 2.5-million-year-old straight-tusked elephant in Beijing, China.

However, it's not just old bones that workers find. In New York City in 2010, excavating operators at the World Trade Center site pulled the earth away from the remains of a late eighteenth-century Dutch ship. A 32-foot (10 m) section of the ship's wooden timbers had lain undisturbed in a landfill more than 20 feet (6 m) below street level until construction of a parking garage began. Construction work in lower Manhattan has often yielded important archaeological discoveries, such as a portion of the city's seventeenth-century fort wall and the colonial-era African Burial Ground, which is now a National Park Service monument.

A Diverse Workforce

Women and minorities are increasingly joining the ranks of heavy equipment operators. Educational opportunities include apprenticeships and training geared specifically for this diverse group. There are also associations and other resources aimed at helping women and minorities develop and further their careers. Women- and minority-owned construction companies are changing the perception of the traditional operator. Also, reasonable accommodations can be made for workers with disabilities.

Women choosing this nontraditional occupation can expect growing support. There is even a Facebook page for female heavy equipment operators. However, in rare instances women might find that male coworkers are not keen on the idea of female operators. Yet, as an article in *Equipment World* titled "Men vs. Women: Who Are the Better Heavy Equipment Operators?" points out, women are clearly proving they have the determination and skills to do well as operators.

chapter 2

Types of Equipment and Environments

Heavy equipment operators are employed in many different types of work environments using all sorts of machines and materials. The gear needed, hours worked, and other factors depend on the requirements of a particular job. Working conditions vary with each location, which can be anything from steep hills to flat roads. Weather plays an important part in how or when a project is handled. Operators sometimes work far away from home, requiring them to stay in temporary housing near the job site. The type and amount of work varies by company and by project, making each job unique and interesting.

Machines and Controls

As cars do, heavy equipment comes in all sizes, makes, and models. Basic groups of machines are track types (similar to bulldozers), excavators, loaders, backhoes, asphalt pavers, and cranes. Tower cranes can reach heights, mobile cranes can be transported, and crawler cranes move on tracks. Hydraulic systems power some machines such as excavators.

Whatever the project or location, there are a number of machines that fit the job:

Heavy equipment includes time- and labor-saving agricultural machines, such as this harvester working a wheat field.

- Backhoes dig or excavate soil and other materials.
- Compactors pack down earth and other materials.
- Drills mine the earth's surface.
- Forest machines load logs onto trucks.
- Harvesters process crops.
- Milling machines prepare roads for resurfacing.
- Mining shovels dig or excavate rock.
- Motor graders prepare flat surfaces.
- Snowplows push and clear away snow.
- Tractors pull agricultural and construction vehicles.
- Trucks transport materials.

One of the largest manufacturers of heavy equipment used in construction and mining is Caterpillar Inc. in the United States. It has several models of the more than three hundred machines that it sells or rents. Other top makers of machinery are Komatsu and Hitachi Construction Machinery based in Japan, Volvo Construction Equipment in Sweden, and Liebherr in Germany. U.S.-based John Deere is the largest manufacturer of agricultural equipment.

How long a piece of heavy equipment will last is based on the work it does and the conditions in which it is operated. Another factor is how well the machinery is maintained. On average, equipment is in operation for ten to twenty years. Depending on funding and cost, project managers may purchase or rent newer models with upgraded technology. The diesel fuel consumption of heavy vehicles varies depending on the workload, but it averages about 10 gallons (38 liters) per hour.

Heavy equipment is driven, guided, and operated using different controls. Operators push pedals and pull levers. They pivot joysticks and valves and turn handwheels like those that move parts to spread wet concrete. Some machines, such as cranes, can be remotely controlled.

MATERIALS AND METHODS

Operators work with many kinds of materials. Some are found at a job site, while others may be trucked in or out for specific purposes. The most obvious is earth or soil. Other commonly used materials are asphalt, concrete, gravel, sand, wood, iron, steel, and stone.

Materials are used to do all manner of tasks—from flat road paving to uneven and hilly terrain work. Clearing, leveling, excavating, loading, dumping, trenching, and grading are usual functions at a project location.

During construction a tower crane sliced through the Sáo Paulo Arena in Brazil, a reminder of how accidents can occur with heavy equipment.

WORK CONDITIONS AND HOURS

Operators work in noisy, dusty, dirty, muddy, greasy environments where the air smells of diesel exhaust from machinery. Possibly hazardous situations exist from traffic, moving equipment, and dangerous materials, such as hot asphalt and chemicals. Any work site, large or small, that uses heavy machines can pose a hazard if safety regulations are overlooked.

Work-related injuries can result from repeated motions, such as pulling levers. Accidents can happen in which heavy equipment overturns and crushes the operator. Cranes collapsing on a building site pose a fatal danger. Sometimes cranes simply fail or errors are made in setting one up. Mishaps are more likely when enormous cranes are squeezed into narrow places like city streets. In New York City, there have been several accidents in which cranes have toppled onto workers and pedestrians below and crashed into nearby buildings. In Brazil, a crane fell over during construction of the São Paulo Arena for the 2014 FIFA World Cup, and two workers were killed.

Among equipment operators on construction sites in the United States, there are approximately twelve deaths per one hundred thousand full-time employees each year, as cited in an article in *Business Insider*. However, the number of injuries and deaths is lower than it was in the last century and continues to drop with the development of safer machines and stricter regulations and inspections.

Weather is a daily consideration on a job site, especially with regards to safety. However, operators may work in all kinds of weather—rain or shine, hot or cold, snow or ice. Weather can be unpredictable and can sometimes lead to heat and cold stress. Wind and rain particularly can delay progress on a project. Most machines can handle all weather conditions. Some equipment cabins are enclosed and have heat and air-conditioning, while others are open and exposed to the elements.

An operator's day starts early, usually about 7 a.m., followed by four to six hours of work, about a thirty-minute lunch break, and then another four to six hours of work. Working hours can be during the day or night and include weekends. A job might require working overtime or in shifts. It's not unusual to work fifty to sixty hours a week to complete a project on time and within budget. Road repair and construction is often carried out at night. Working overnight avoids daytime traffic jams and keeps the crew safer since there are fewer vehicles on the road. Extreme weather conditions, such as snowstorms or heat waves, can result in a temporary work stoppage.

What to Wear

Wearing the right clothing for the job helps keep heavy equipment operators protected and safe. By following the regulations of the Occupational Safety & Health Administration (OSHA)

Workers constructing a concrete road in downtown Denver, Colorado, are outfitted with the proper safety attire, including hard hats, gloves, boots, and reflective vests.

DIGGING FOR FUN

Mention the words "theme park," and most people think of the iconic Disneyland or Walt Disney World or the newer Wizarding World of Harry Potter. But a construction-themed adventure park? Could there be such a thing? There is! And it's called Diggerland USA.

Diggerland USA opened in 2014 in West Berlin, New Jersey, and offers twenty-three attractions across 14 acres (6 hectares). Visitors can ride, drive, and work heavy machinery in a safe, supervised setting. Sitting in the cab of a 14,515-pound (6,584-kilogram) giant digger lets kids of all ages learn what it's like to operate heavy equipment. Amusement park rides, like the Spin Dizzy and Sky Shuttle, are also part of the fun.

Diggerland was founded in the United Kingdom, with the first park opening in 2000. There are now four there, with a fifth one planned.

and the Federal Highway Administration, operators and their employers can help prevent accidents and injuries. Clothing requirements vary by the work performed and the location of the job. Safety gear that protects workers from head to toe is the best bet, as is avoiding loose-fitting clothes that can get caught in machinery.

The hard hat is the most familiar and important piece of occupational safety attire for operators. Gloves and thick boots help protect against machinery mishaps and some weather conditions. Earplugs protect hearing from the loud cranking of machinery. Goggles keep eyes shielded from work site debris and weather.

Some jobs or work locations require additional and specialized gear, such as face masks or breathing apparatuses to protect airways and aid breathing. Reflective or high-visibility vests and other clothing, especially when worn at night, let other operators and drivers in the area take notice of workers on a site.

WORKING ON LOCATION

An interesting aspect of an operator's career is working at new or different locations for each job. Employment might be found close to home or require commuting long distances. Working at a remote location means staying days, weeks, or months to finish the job or a portion of it. Workers who are flexible and mobile stand a better chance of being regularly employed.

Large projects draw experienced workers from near and far. When there are not enough local skilled workers, employers recruit them from out of town. Mohawk Indians traveled each week from the Kahnawake reserve near Quebec, Canada, to work on One World Trade Center in New York City, spending weekends at home. The New NY Bridge in Tarrytown, New York, included operators from as far as California. Operators from Texas and Oklahoma filled out the construction ranks during a labor shortage in San Francisco.

WORKING WITH AND FOR CLIENTS

Some employment opportunities for heavy equipment operators are client based. An established company holds the contract on a specific job and hires operators for the length of the project or a portion of it. For example, at Colonial Williamsburg, in Williamsburg, Virginia, operators were hired to use excavators and dump trucks to prepare the foundation for the reconstruction of the Market House.

Building of the New NY Bridge is overseen by the design-builder Tappan Zee Constructors, which is made up of four

The I Lift NY super crane positions one of many massive steel girders on the road deck of the New NY Bridge in Tarrytown, New York.

companies. In order to complete this massive project on time and on budget, Tappan Zee Constructors also hires many subcontractors to assist. Subcontractors are businesses that do work for a larger company or on a particular project. They often fulfill many aspects of the assignment and hire qualified operators to do the work. Maintaining a good relationship with the client is essential to job progress and a pleasant working environment.

chapter 3

Duties and Responsibilities

The particular location and type of job determines the methods used to complete a project. Building a bridge and raising a high rise require different methods of construction but use similar pieces of heavy equipment. Specialized work, like pile driving, needs operators with specific skills. All kinds of projects benefit from employees who have good communication skills and practice teamwork. Above all, keeping up with the latest safety rules and regulations, plus being trustworthy and responsible, makes heavy equipment operators effective in their work.

Different Locations, Different Tasks

Heavy equipment operation covers a wide range of jobs at a wide range of locations. Operators work on bridges and dams, roads and highways, and houses and skyscrapers. Commercial agriculture and smaller farms depend on large machines and their operators. Railway maintenance, mining, and forestry also use variations of heavy equipment. While some equipment and methods may be used across project sites, each type of work has specific requirements.

Building roads and highways involves earthmoving with large excavators. This is called rough grading. It is followed by

The forestry industry uses heavy equipment like this feller buncher mounted on tracks, which gathers and cuts fir trees at a logging operation in Oregon.

a finer grading of the site. Next comes surfacing with a choice of materials such as asphalt, concrete, gravel, or a combination of them. Compacting surfacing materials well is an important skill for a heavy equipment operator. The better the road is compacted, the longer the life of the road or highway.

Mining uses many of the same machines needed to construct highways and roads, such as excavators and bulldozers. Surface mining requires a mass excavator. Underground mining uses smaller equipment designed for tight spaces. Forestry also has some form of heavy equipment suited to logging.

Delimbers are attached to hydraulic excavators and strip the branches from felled trees. Feller bunchers are fastened to a heavy equipment base and can cut and gather several trees.

Agriculture has its own heavy equipment for plowing, planting, and harvesting crops. Tractors are multifunctional machines able to haul other equipment needed in farming. Combines harvest crops like wheat, oats, and corn. They combine the processes of reaping, threshing, and winnowing in one time-saving process. Modern combines have hydraulic steering and air-conditioned cabs. Sprayers are used to apply fertilizers and pesticides to crops. Small sprayers are tractor drawn, while larger motorized ones have spray booms nearly 150 feet (46 m) long.

Building and maintaining railroads requires equipment that runs on rails. Railroad ties are supported by a ballast of crushed stone. Ballast regulators form and distribute the ballast. Tamping machines then pack down the ballast that is underneath the rails to make the tracks stronger. Lining machines adjust the alignment and level of the rails.

An unpleasant but necessary and useful task for heavy equipment operators is recovery work at natural disaster sites. Hurricanes, tornadoes, floods, and mudslides result in chaotic scenes of torn and twisted debris. Operators use all types of large machines—such as bulldozers, front-end loaders, dump trucks, and forklifts—to clear the mangled mess and haul it away. Clearing roads is especially important so that emergency vehicles can get through.

Disaster locations are dangerous and unpredictable, requiring highly skilled workers who follow OSHA guidelines. Operators were on the job after Hurricane Katrina hit New Orleans in 2005. Crane operators lifted cars lying across the tracks following the 2015 Amtrak derailment in Philadelphia.

A railcar is lifted by crane from the accident site following a train derailment in northern India.

SPECIALIZED WORK

Within the field of heavy equipment operation, there are complex tasks that require specific training and skills. Operators with expert knowledge of a particular job or machine make up a smaller part of the workforce. They use hydraulic cranes, telescopic booms, rough-terrain trucks, drillers, and pile drivers.

Pile drivers—like those used to build the New NY Bridge in Tarrytown, New York—are set on barges or cranes to pound piles into the ground for foundations. Piles are long, heavy supporting beams made of steel or concrete. Pile-driver operators use various types of pile drivers from large to small and work on offshore oil rigs, piers, and building foundations.

COMMUNICATION SKILLS

Operating heavy equipment obviously is not an office job. So then why are good communication abilities a career requirement? Possessing basic reading, writing, and verbal skills is essential for operators in order to follow through on jobs and for career development.

Surprisingly, there is lots of material for operators to read on and about the job, such as maps, diagrams, charts, and specifications. They need to consult equipment manuals and check machine inspection forms. Reading comprehension is especially important for understanding the contents in safety and hazardous material procedures sheets. Information distributed by employers comes in the form of work orders, memos, and bulletins.

Decent writing skills are needed on a daily basis. Operators write a record of each day's work activities. They also fill out forms, such as for machine maintenance. Written tests are part of advanced training on heavy equipment.

Sharing information in an uncomplicated manner is key to strong verbal skills. Operators need to give easily

THE LEFT COAST LIFTER

Imagine a crane that's more than thirty stories tall. Next, imagine it lifting twelve Statues of Liberty or about 2,000 tons (1,814 metric tonnes). The Left Coast Lifter is that tall and that strong. This mammoth crane, one of the largest in the world, sits on a 384-foot (117-m) floating barge. Its boom measures 328 feet (100 m).

The Left Coast Lifter was first used to replace a span of the San Francisco–Oakland Bay Bridge that was damaged by a 1989 earthquake. After completing that project, the massive crane made a 1,600-mile (2,575-kilometer) journey from California through the Panama Canal and up the East Coast to Tarrytown, New York, to construct a new bridge and demolish the old one.

Nicknamed I Lift NY for its New York assignment, the crane can lift more than 1,900 tons (1,724 t) at one time, including 1,000-ton (907-t) sections of the new bridge. Parts of the bridge can be built on nearby water barges and lifted right into place rather than having to be transported from other construction sites on land. Ron Burgess is a third-generation crane operator working the super crane. According to an article in the *Journal News*, Burgess told Khurram Saeed, "It's a very dangerous job and you always have to double- and triple-check yourself when you're doing something."

understood instructions and directions on a job assignment. Explanations of equipment problems should be clear to coworkers and supervisors. Conducting a group discussion on how to proceed on a part of a project promotes good teamwork and cooperation. Communication on a noisy job site includes shouting above the roar of machines and using hand signals and handheld radios.

Teamwork

Ever wonder why there are so many workers on a job site? Most projects that use heavy equipment require several men and women working as a team under a crew leader or supervisor. Together they get the job done safely, on time, and within budget. For example, while one operator sits in the cab on a loader or crane, coworkers might communicate special instructions by handheld radios.

However, sometimes an individual will be responsible for one part of a job and will work alone to accomplish that task. Being able to follow through with little or no supervision is an important skill to develop and one that carries great responsibility.

Safety Rules and Regulations

The most important aspect of a heavy equipment operator's work is following health and safety rules and regulations. Being up to date on industry standards—like those enforced by OSHA—can help prevent hazardous situations and potential injuries. Safety and maintenance checks should be performed on large equipment on a daily basis, along with cleaning and minor repairs as needed. Machines must have working brakes, headlights, taillights, and seatbelts. Equipment should be used only for its intended purpose and not overloaded. Vehicles that need maintenance or repairs or have defective parts must be reported to a supervisor. Only workers who have been trained on specific machines should operate those pieces of equipment.

Watching one's personal safety, as well as that of the work team or others around, is key to maintaining a secure job site. A basic knowledge of first aid is helpful, and continuing education and training in safety procedures is necessary, too.

During a U.S. Army exercise at Fort Chaffee, Arkansas, a job site supervisor instructs a heavy equipment operator training on a motorized road grader.

Environmental hazards, such as extreme weather or exposure to toxic substances, should be avoided. However, despite every precaution taken at job sites, accidents do happen while using heavy equipment.

An OSHA representative and heavy equipment operators discuss the safety hazards they might encounter during cleanup following a tornado in Washington, Illinois.

Essential Qualities

There are other vital characteristics that make for valuable heavy equipment operators. By paying attention to details, observing their environment, and thinking ahead, operators can improve the workspace for themselves and coworkers. Employers and coworkers appreciate working with operators who are trustworthy, responsible, and results oriented. Also, those operators who welcome new challenges and learning opportunities find that those traits aid in advancing their careers.

chapter 4

TRAINING AND SKILLS

Before choosing a career or starting out in one, it's important to determine if the interest in it is real or a passing curiosity. The next step is finding out if there's a strong enough capability for learning the work and making it a lifelong vocation. The study of heavy equipment includes several topics. Instruction is given in the basics of machine operation, as well as related subjects like safety precautions. Future operators can choose to learn through accredited schools, unions, or on-the-job training. In many cases, crane operators must earn a license or certification. Heavy machine operation is a strenuous occupation. It requires stamina and skills, such as quick thinking and sharp reflexes.

DETERMINING APTITUDE

Aptitude is a natural or learned ability to function in a certain capacity. Finding out if an aptitude exists for any occupation involves believing in the talent to learn the work and finding out as much as possible about it. The Internet provides ample information on the numerous types of large machines and how to operate them. Reading about and watching videos of

Students taking courses in auto mechanics and mechanical engineering can find the information they learned useful when beginning to train in heavy equipment operation.

heavy equipment operation can help determine if the career is a good fit.

AREAS OF STUDY

Once a career is settled on, it's time to chart a plan of study. Most heavy equipment training programs require a high school or vocational-technical (vo-tech) education or its equivalent. The U.S. Bureau of Labor Statistics (BLS) cites the secondary school subjects English, math, and shop as being useful in this career. It also mentions that a course in auto mechanics would be helpful since many operators perform regular maintenance on the machines they use.

Setting out to study heavy equipment operation offers several options. Choosing the right school or training program depends on current social and personal circumstances as well as long-term goals. Heavy equipment instruction is offered by some colleges and community colleges, leading to an associate's degree. Training is also supplied by technical and trade schools, certified training programs, and unions like the International Union of Operating Engineers (IUOE). It's important to check the accreditation of a school or training course before beginning any studies.

Specific courses in equipment training vary with each school or program. Generally, they cover start-up and shutdown procedures, controls and gauges, preoperational and postoperational equipment inspections, and loading, hauling, dumping, digging, and grading. Instruction includes classroom hours and learning to operate the big machines in the field and by computer simulation. New technology in equipment, such as computerized controls, requires some understanding of and training in electronics. Communication in the workplace and OSHA training are also course requirements.

Types of Training

The need for competent heavy equipment operators has created several training resources from which to choose. Many operators start their careers with on-the-job training. They work with experienced equipment operators, learning to use smaller machines before driving larger ones, such as bulldozers.

Job prospects are better for those who enter an apprenticeship program. Over the course of three or four years, an apprentice must take a set number of hours of technical instruction along with paid on-the-job training. Apprentices are considered journeymen or journeywomen upon completing the program and can operate a wider variety of machinery with less guidance. From there they can work their way up to foreman or forewoman. Apprenticeships are offered by unions, training schools, and some state-sponsored programs. Waiting lists are not uncommon for apprenticeships, so it's best to apply early.

Union training is offered at local branches of the IUOE in the United States and Canada. Most union apprenticeship programs are recognized by state and federal agencies. For the operator hopeful who has little knowledge of this trade, this is an excellent place to begin. The IUOE lists starting pay for apprentices as 45 to 60 percent of a journeyperson's wages. Jobs are assigned for all union members based on how long they have been unemployed. The IUOE takes part in a Job Corps program for training young people ages sixteen to twenty-four. Training with a union is beneficial since many large commercial construction projects are unionized. Operators of mobile, tower, and overhead cranes can earn certification through the IUOE's Operating Engineers Certification Program (OECP). This program evaluates the abilities of crane operators, thereby assuring a safe work environment. Crane operators can also

An army heavy equipment operator at Fort Hunter Liggett, California, prepares a lot for paving by spreading soil with a motorized road grader.

receive certification from the National Commission for the Certification of Crane Operators (NCCCO), which is offered by some equipment training schools.

Joining the U.S. Army is another way to learn heavy equipment operation. The military needs qualified operators on army construction projects and supplies the training. Applicants first take the Armed Services Vocational Aptitude Battery test, which determines if a military position is the best fit. Next is ten weeks of basic combat instruction followed by nine weeks of Advanced Individual Training (AIT). This includes classroom and field work with heavy machines.

Depending on the state, licenses or certifications are sometimes needed to operate equipment such as bulldozers, loaders, backhoes, cranes, and pile drivers. Many states require operators to have a commercial driver's licenses in order to transport equipment on public roads to job sites. Equipment operators who

OPERATOR TRAINING FOR WOMEN

More women are now breaking into nontraditional jobs, including heavy equipment operation. While not exactly new to the field, women still make up only a small percentage of operators. In the United States, women account for about 2 percent of equipment operators, according to the BLS. Service Canada lists the number at

More women are joining the ranks of heavy equipment operators, as demonstrated by this woman sitting at the controls of an earth-moving machine.

about 1.5 percent. Women with families find that operating some equipment, such as dump trucks, which are usually driven during the day, allows enough time for raising a family while providing a good paycheck.

Some women start out in the construction sector by directing traffic around a work site and learning on the job. Other women attend heavy equipment training schools, many of which are actively recruiting women. Hawkeye Community College in Waterloo, Iowa, offers a ten-day heavy equipment operator training program specifically for women and minorities.

A 2013 Tradeswomen Survey, conducted by the Institute for Women's Policy Research, described what women experience in the construction job sector. Some women followed family into the trade, as one woman said she worked with her father. Others found information about the field in various ways, including ads and flyers. Another woman said she has "a passion for driving and equipment operation." Nearly 30 percent of women responded in the survey that they were the only female on a job site. Thirty percent also reported gender harassment. One woman noted, "There is usually at least one jerk per job, but the majority of my coworkers are decent humans."

While opportunities are widening for women in equipment operation, challenges still exist in finding adequate training and remaining employed. Apprenticeships, however, are expected to double over the next five years following President Obama's 2014 announcement of a $100 million jobs initiative.

hold additional credentials are more prepared to enter the workforce in a range of areas.

Graduates of heavy equipment training can become union members or become self-employed. They can select to work in the public or private sector—that is, at local or state government agencies or at individually owned construction firms. Experienced heavy equipment operators can choose to teach at a training facility or school. Their mastery of these large machines assists new operators in developing skills that will lead to satisfying employment.

PHYSICAL REQUIREMENTS

Every career has physical demands, whether it's standing for long periods of time or sitting in the cramped cab of a 22-ton (20-t) tower crane nearly 400 feet (122 m) in the air. In general, heavy equipment operators need good balance and excellent hand-to-eye-to-foot coordination. Good eyesight and depth perception are necessary in order to judge distances between objects when maneuvering large machines. Most important, operators should be able to display a fast reaction time with quick reflexes around moving equipment.

Equipment operators also need adequate strength for pushing, pulling, and lifting heavy loads without getting winded. Working at heights without fear is essential, especially for crane operators. While these physical requirements might seem demanding, an easygoing attitude can make them feel effortless.

ADDITIONAL ABILITIES

There are other skills that heavy equipment operators rely on each day. Mechanical aptitude lets operators keep in tune with the complex machines they run. Knowing how to detect issues before they become problems keeps machines and workers safe on the job site. Obviously, excellent driving skills are expected of operators since they maneuver heavy equipment.

A strong comprehension of verbal directions and written instructions assures that operators will carry out their portion of a project's plan. Staying up to date on current and developing technology in large machines is an ongoing part of an operator's career. A seemingly small but equally important skill is managing time effectively so that the work gets done as scheduled. Sometimes, this also means being flexible as timetables change.

chapter 5

Landing That First Job and Keeping It

Searching for a first job can be an anxious experience in any field or career. Having the right qualifications for the work is a good start. Job hunting involves researching companies that offer desirable employment opportunities. A strong cover letter and résumé can help land interviews, and getting ready to meet a prospective employer takes some preparation. Even after landing that first job, it's never too early to explore ways to get ahead in a new career.

Getting Started

Finding a job is a job in itself. It takes time, patience, and research. To start an employment search, the best thing to do is find out which companies are hiring and for which positions.

Web-based job hunting is the easiest and most common way to find out what opportunities are available and where. Employment details are listed on websites such as WowJobs.ca, Workopolis.com, simplyhired.ca, MONSTER.com, and indeed.com. Overseas openings as far away as New Zealand

Equipment operators looking for work meet with prospective employers at a job fair in Washington, D.C.

can be found on goabroad.com. Operators with disabilities can check for work on disabledperson.com.

Job fairs or forums bring together operators looking for work and employers looking to hire. Interviews are conducted at a given time and location. Information on job fairs is found on employment websites.

Exploring local companies is another option. Long-established businesses that specialize in specific work, like excavating, might have openings for local equipment operators. Investigate current or up-and-coming neighborhood construction projects for employment. Approach regional or municipal organizations, such as departments of work, to find job possibilities.

Operator training schools and unions often provide personalized career counseling and employment assistance. This can include leads on jobs and listings of employers who are hiring. Counselors help match the best candidate with a particular position in a desired geographical region. Additional guidance is offered on how to apply for work, résumé preparation, and interviewing techniques so that operators can spotlight their skills.

RÉSUMÉ AND COVER LETTER

Every trade or profession requires a résumé and a cover letter for job searches and career development and advancement. A résumé is a record of qualifications and accomplishments at each level or stage of an occupation. Prospective employers need to see résumés in order to hire the equipment operator best suited for a particular job opening.

An entry-level résumé starts with educational background, including relevant courses and any related work experience. Listing part-time employment, internships, apprenticeships, certifications, and formal training gives a fuller picture of a prospective employee's abilities. For a heavy equipment operator with several years of experience, the résumé is a record of the types of machines used and under which conditions. The operator might list equipment, like a Cat grader, and note how it was used in building a specific roadway. Other items to mention are additional training and commendations for outstanding work.

Writing a résumé might seem challenging. Some operator training schools offer assistance with composing a résumé. A web presence is also helpful in employment and career advancement. Operators can assemble an electronic portfolio, or e-portfolio, of their achievements. Developing a personal profile on a professional networking website, such as LinkedIn, is also popular.

It might seem that a cover letter is needless when there's a résumé. However, the cover letter is an introduction to the résumé and the job candidate. It should interest potential employers enough to continue on to read the résumé. A cover letter can include other information less suited to a résumé format, such as work-related skills and other interests that reveal a bit about the applicant's personality. Most important to include is why the candidate is interested in the position and is the right match. Crafting a strong résumé and cover letter shows employers a potential applicant's ability to communicate well with supervisors, coworkers, and clients.

Interview Process

When an applicant receives a phone call or email from an interested employer, it's time to do some homework. Preparing for an interview is like studying for an exam. Research the company and the job, and go into the interview knowing about how the business works. Wear casual but neat clothing.

CONSTRUCTION ON TV

Want to know about the largest or most newsworthy construction projects? One way to find out what heavy equipment operators are working on worldwide is to tune in to ConstructionCamTV. This website streams live multiple camera views of ongoing work around the globe. It's part of EarthCam.net, which provides webcam scenes of unique destinations as well as popular ones like the Statue of Liberty and the Eiffel Tower.

ConstructionCamTV counts businesses, government agencies, and tourism among its customers. It is designed primarily to help project leaders and managers monitor their construction sites without having to leave their offices. They can track their teams' minute-by-minute progress and document the entire building process. Just as important, the webcams also help promote public awareness of ongoing construction ventures by demonstrating the many stages that make up these projects.

The latest construction sites—in transportation, industries, tourism, the energy sector, arenas, stadiums, and college campuses—can be viewed twenty-four hours a day in all time zones. Especially fascinating to watch is the large-scale development of the Qatar Rail Project in Southwest Asia. Construction enthusiasts can follow the building of this public transit system that will haul passengers and freight across Qatar. Other major construction projects documented are the San Francisco–Oakland Bay Bridge, Hong Kong Disneyland, and the Canadian Museum for Human Rights in Winnipeg.

There are also vintage construction images and time-lapse photos. The 9/11 Memorial Museum Tribute time lapse tracks construction from the first trucks rolling in to boom cranes swinging across the Manhattan sky.

A boom crane helps workers position the tower on the Sleeping Beauty Castle at the Hong Kong Disneyland.

Be prepared to answer questions about education and related experience. Employers usually ask applicants how their background has prepared them for the job opening. More specific information could be asked about safety skills

A heavy equipment instructor trains two women in the use of a residential snowplow in Denver, Colorado.

and working under certain conditions and schedules. Many interviewers ask candidates why they are the best person for the job, why they want the position, and why they should be hired. Interviewees cannot be discriminated against because of age, race, or gender.

Answer questions truthfully at an interview because once you're in the operator's seat, work performance will reveal any misinformation. The interview process can include additional meetings as candidates for a job are narrowed down. If employment is offered on the spot at the end of an interview, be sure it's the right fit before accepting it. Applicants may also be asked to submit to medical exams, random drug and/or alcohol testing, and background checks. Finally, relax and learn from the interview experience so that the next one becomes easier.

Getting In

Most everyone starts at the bottom of the employment ladder with entry-level work. Heavy equipment operators must be at least eighteen years of age, possess a high school diploma or have passed a general education development (GED) test, and have a valid driver's license. Some types of jobs call for specialized courses or certification. Operating a dump truck, for example, requires a commercial driver's license. Prior work experience might be a requirement for some employment.

Many operators, including women, start out as laborers on a project site to get the overall picture of what goes on. They learn on the job or then get into an apprentice-training program. However, heavy equipment operators are divided on the need for formal instruction. Some operators believe that on-the-job training offers the best education. In the United States and Canada, operator hopefuls can choose from ninety-five local apprenticeship and training programs sponsored by the IUOE. Nonunion employment is another possible starting point.

Getting Ahead

Starting at the bottom of the employment ladder leaves several rungs to climb over the span of a career. One way to make progress as a heavy equipment operator is to learn as much as possible on the job and show an interest in moving forward. Another way is by taking advanced, specialized, and supplemental training. Updating skills and knowledge, like learning new safety procedures, is also helpful.

Operators can advance toward a supervisory position with added responsibilities. Beginning first as apprentices, operators expand their knowledge of equipment usage to work their way up to journeypersons, operators, and finally foremen or

forewomen. Some types of work require a certain number of years of experience before an operator can apply for the position. Other jobs involve specialized training, such as operating a wheel trencher used to dig trenches for laying pipes.

Keeping up with coworkers through social networking helps equipment operators find out about new jobs and other information that can advance career goals. Training schools and unions often provide access to and suggestions on networking. Total Resources Network is a top networking site that brings together personnel in the skilled trades by posting information about job seekers, employment openings, and training opportunities.

chapter 6

Future Outlook

At the beginning of a career it's hard to know what the future holds. Enjoying the work is most important. However, the long-term question is whether there will be enough employment opportunities in the coming years. Projections of job availability and growth should be taken into consideration before embarking on a chosen career. Yet, employment projections about the labor market can vary over time. All occupations experience highs and lows, with the demand for workers often affected by changes in the economy and other social factors. Heavy equipment operation is expected to maintain mostly steady growth for the next several years. Staying competitive and one step ahead of what employers want from operators is key to developing a rewarding and enduring career.

Operators lift a car by crane from the rubble of the Skagit River bridge collapse in Mount Vernon, Washington.

JOB GROWTH

Working in a field that offers personal satisfaction is the goal of most employees. It's an added benefit if that career is expected to experience above-average job growth. For heavy equipment operators, employment is on the rise, especially in the construction sector. The U.S. BLS forecasts that demand for excavating and loading machine operators and crane operators is expected to increase 17 percent by 2022, especially for computerized crane operators. The BLS puts job growth for all other equipment operators at 21 percent through 2022. That's more than double the job increase across all other occupations. Service Canada lists the outlook for equipment operator jobs there as fair, except in mining.

Certain sectors of heavy equipment operation offer more employment opportunities. The timber industry needs operators for harvesting machines. According to an article in the *Green Bay Press-Gazette*, Mark Huempfner told Richard Ryman, "For equipment operators, it seems like an ongoing process trying to find good, qualified people." In North Dakota in particular, more housing construction, brought on by a population increase with the oil boom, has opened doors for operators.

America's aging infrastructure—roads, bridges, railways, and utilities—is overdue for maintenance and repair. The American Society of Civil Engineers gave it a D+ in its 2013 report card and estimated that an investment of $3.6 trillion is needed for improvements. A *USA Today* article cited a Federal Highway Administration report that stated that 11 percent of bridges are unsound. In May 2013, Interstate Highway 5 collapsed over the Skagit River in Washington State. Construction of the New NY Bridge in Tarrytown, New York, was sped up to replace the deteriorating Tappan Zee Bridge. The urgent work on infrastructure could increase job demand for heavy equipment operators by 20 percent over the next several years. However, bureaucratic delays and cuts in government budgets could slow this employment growth.

Job Statistics

Salary ranges for operators vary by geographical location, project, and the machine operated. Pile-driver operators and other highly trained equipment operators earn higher wages. Apprentices earn 60 to 70 percent of a fully trained operator's salary. Wages are projected to grow with the demand for operators. Up-to-date figures and information can be found on the BLS website.

Overall, heavy equipment operators enjoy competitive salaries. Depending on their employer, operators have good benefits, such as health insurance, life insurance, disability insurance, retirement and pension programs, and vacation and holiday pay. In comparison to other occupations, a higher percentage of operators belong to a union.

Job satisfaction is high among equipment operators. They like the work, and there is little turnover. In fact, there are generations of operators with sons and daughters following in a parent's career path. However, as more operators near retirement age, there will be a need for highly trained workers to enter the field. Minorities and women can expect more opportunities in both training and jobs. Presently, the BLS lists minority employment at 6.8 percent African American, 16.9 percent Hispanic or Latino, and 0.1 percent Asian.

Getting High Tech

Technology is changing and improving the way heavy equipment is operated. Manufacturers of large machines are constantly updating and developing safer and more

A worker determines the GPS coordinates on a section of natural gas pipeline before it is positioned in a trench in Howell, Michigan.

computerized equipment. In the past ten years, equipment controls have become more complex yet simpler to use as they help operators do a more precise job. In a *Wall Street Journal* article, industry consultant Frank Manfredi told James R. Hagerty, "Everybody is trying to make these machines easier to operate because it's harder and harder to find people with the required skills."

A Global Positioning System (GPS) allows operators to bulldoze a section of earth to within a fraction of an inch based on a computer-generated plan. For example, Komatsu has developed a 41,000-pound (18,597 kg) bulldozer, worth nearly half a million dollars, in which operators are guided by small computers in the cabin. Monitors show how the bulldozer's 13-foot (4-m) blade cuts into the soil, as well as general information about the machine's performance.

Improvements in hydraulic steering systems reduce consumption of fuel and increase machine efficiency. Decreased operator fatigue and improved safety are added benefits of this new form of equipment steering. Telematics hardware is making it possible for employers and project managers to track how a piece of heavy equipment is being operated at a remote location. It's a wireless technology that sends, receives, and stores information. In an article in *Equipment World*, Allen Feller discussed the advantages of having telematics on his fleet of Caterpillar excavators. Feller told Wayne Grayson that through telematics technology, he learned that "one of my drivers is popping that truck out of gear."

These days there's an app for nearly everything, including heavy equipment. The Heavy Equipment Inspection app enables operators to conduct thorough daily safety checks of machines on the job site. Using lists and forms customized on smartphones and tablets, the app saves time on machine inspections and cuts down on wasteful paperwork.

High-tech training is turning out high-tech operators. Wake Tech in Raleigh, North Carolina, has a high-tech training program that uses simulators for instructing heavy equipment operators. Learning on simulators of backhoes, bulldozers, and excavators, rather than on actual heavy machinery, is safer and less costly. It also helps students strengthen hand-eye-foot coordination and practice precise movements. In a Wake Tech news release, department head Ronnie Lowe said, "These simulators will provide the hands-on training students need to build those skills and become proficient." A mobile simulator classroom is being planned at Assiniboine Community College in Manitoba, Canada. These latest technologies are also part of training courses provided by the IUOE.

Staying Competitive

Entering the job market is just the beginning of a career. However, staying actively employed also takes work. It means

GOING GREEN

The heavy equipment industry is going green. What does that mean? Green jobs are performed in a way that preserves and even improves the quality of the environment. Specifically, these jobs cut down on pollution and waste, such as carbon emissions from fossil fuels. In equipment operation, it means operators follow onsite green procedures such as removing and recycling construction materials and waste.

Operating a several thousand–pound trencher that digs ditches for sewer or utility lines ordinarily requires exceptional care. On a green job site, workers might be controlling this kind of machinery near an environmentally sensitive location, such as a watershed or an environmentally protected zone. In this case, extra measures are taken to prevent damage and to safeguard the area.

The demand for green jobs and the highly trained operators who can handle them is on the rise. Training for the green construction sector is offered by equipment career schools like Associated Training Services (ATS) and the College of Instrument Technology (CIT). According to the BLS, "Depending on the type of equipment, the operator may be required to be certified by an accredited party or by the manufacturer."

In 2007, the Green Jobs Initiative was launched. In 2010, the BLS began collecting new data on green jobs. Currently, it does not have information on wages earned by operators in the green construction industry.

knowing how to be of value to employers. It also means knowing how to develop skills that aid in climbing the employment ladder. An employee who can build on strengths and work on weaknesses will be an asset to any company and be able to advance his or her career.

glossary

apprenticeship A position of employment for a set time during which a worker is instructed by a professional in the field.

benefits Compensation offered by an employer in addition to a salary.

certification Documentation that proves certain standards have been met in order to do a specific job.

entry-level Describes a beginning position within a field of work or at a company.

foreman/forewoman Someone who leads and supervises workers.

Global Positioning System (GPS) A satellite-based navigation system that can determine geographic location.

grading A process by which a road is prepared for construction by building a level base or a specified slope.

hydraulic system The use of liquids circulating in a confined space under pressure in order to power machines.

infrastructure The framework of buildings, bridges, roads, and rails that make up a community.

journeyperson An individual who has finished an apprenticeship of a certain trade but is not yet a master of it.

joystick An upright handheld tool that can be moved in several directions to control a device or machine.

networking A process of connecting with people to exchange ideas and information.

remote location A place that is far away from a person's home or from the general population.

simulator A machine that imitates an actual situation or environment and is used in training and research.

specification A detailed illustration of a design used to create or assemble something.

subcontractor A person or company that is hired to perform a portion of a larger project.

trenching The process of digging a deep, long, and usually narrow hole for construction purposes such as laying down pipes and wires.

union An organization of workers formed to protect the interests of its members.

for more information

International Union of Operating Engineers (IUOE)
1125 17th Street NW
Washington, DC 20036
(202) 429-9100
Website: http://www.iuoe.org
The IUOE is a diverse trade union that has represented its members' interests since 1896. Heavy equipment operators make up a large number of the IUOE's membership, along with other construction trades. More than 120 local unions of the IUOE are located in the United States and Canada.

IUOE Canada
350 Sparks Street, Suite 1102
Ottawa, ON K1R 7S8
Canada
(613) 567-5544
Website: http://www.iuoe.org/about-iuoe/iuoe-canada
The Canadian branch of the IUOE provides information of specific interest to Canadian workers.

National Association of Women in Construction (NAWIC)
327 S. Adams Street
Fort Worth, TX 76104
(817) 877-5551
Website: http://www.nawic.org
Founded in 1953 by women working in construction, NAWIC is a support network that provides professional development, education, and networking services for its members. NAWIC has nearly two hundred chapters across

the United States and partners with organizations to help women develop successful careers in construction.

NCCER (formerly called National Center for Construction Education and Research)
13614 Progress Boulevard
Alachua, FL 32615
(888) 622-3720
Website: http://www.nccer.org
Since 1996, NCCER has transformed and standardized training for the construction industry. NCCER offers training, assessment, and an online curriculum to help build a skilled workforce.

North American Heavy Equipment Training Services (NAHETS)
199 North Arroyo Grande Boulevard, Suite 150
Henderson, NV 89074
(888) 879-9492
Website: http://nahets.org
NAHETS is a resource organization that focuses on instructing heavy equipment and crane operators at the entry level. Training, specialized instruction, and certification are offered to develop highly skilled operators who exceed the industry's standards.

Occupational Safety & Health Administration (OSHA)
U.S. Department of Labor
200 Constitution Avenue NW
Washington, DC 20210
(800) 321-OSHA (6742)
Website: https://www.osha.gov
Since 1970, OSHA has been ensuring that work environments of all kinds are healthy and safe by setting specific

standards. OSHA provides training for workers to recognize and prevent dangers on the job site.

Women Building Futures Society (WBF)
10326 107 Street NW
Edmonton, AB T5J 1K2
Canada
(780) 452-1200
Website: http://www.womenbuildingfutures.com
This organization recruits, trains, and supports women in the heavy trades. Created in 1998, WBF has also empowered Aboriginal women to build careers in nontraditional occupations.

Websites

Because of the changing nature of Internet links, Rosen Publishing has developed an online list of websites related to the subject of this book. This site is updated regularly. Please use this link to access this list:

http://www.rosenlinks.com/ECAR/Heavy

for further reading

Browning, Edgar A. *Roadbuilding Construction Equipment at Work: Building the Early Interstate Highways through New England's Green Mountain.* Hudson, WI: Enthusiast Books, 2001.

Byers, Ann. *Jobs as Green Builders and Planners.* New York, NY: Rosen Publishing, 2010.

Capachi, Nick, and John Capachi. *Excavation and Grading Handbook.* Carlsbad, CA: Craftsman Book Company, 2005.

Davis, Michael D. *Coal Mining Equipment at Work: Featuring the World Famous Mines and Mining Companies of Western Kentucky.* Hudson, WI: Enthusiast Books, 2011.

Haddock, Keith. *Bucyrus Heavy Equipment Construction and Mining Machines, 1880–2008: A Photo Gallery.* Hudson, WI: Enthusiast Books, 2008.

Jackson, Barbara J. *Construction Management Jump Start: The Best First Step Toward a Career in Construction Management.* Hoboken, NJ: Sybex, 2010.

Klancher, Lee. *The Art of the John Deere Tractor.* Minneapolis, MN: Voyageur Press, 2011.

Leavitt, Amie Jane. *The Vo-Tech Track to Success in Architecture and Construction* (Learning a Trade, Preparing for a Career). New York, NY: Rosen Publishing, 2015.

Masters, Nancy Robinson. *Heavy Equipment Operator.* North Mankato, MN: Cherry Lake Publishing, 2010.

NCCER. *Heavy Equipment Operations, Level 1 Trainee Guide.* Upper Saddle River, NJ: Prentice Hall, 2012.

Nichols, Herbert, and David Day. *Moving the Earth: The Workbook of Excavation.* 6th ed. New York, NY: McGraw-Hill Professional, 2010.

Orlemann, Eric C. *Modern LeTourneau Earthmoving Equipment: 1968–Present.* Hudson, WI: Enthusiast Books, 2013.

Orlemann, Eric C. *R. G. LeTourneau Heavy Equipment: The Mechanical Drive Era, 1921–1953.* Hudson, WI: Enthusiast Books, 2009.

Orlemann, Eric C. *R. G. LeTourneau Heavy Equipment Photo Gallery.* Hudson, WI: Enthusiast Books, 2014.

Passbooks. *Heavy Equipment Operator.* Syosset, NY: National Learning Corporation, 2014.

Raczon, Frank, and Keith Haddock. *Caterpillar: Modern Earthmoving Marvels.* Minneapolis, MN: Motorbooks, 2015.

Stout, Glenn, Charles Vitchers, and Robert Gray. *Nine Months at Ground Zero: The Story of the Brotherhood of Workers Who Took on a Job like No Other.* New York, NY: Scribner, 2006.

Weitzman, David. *Skywalkers: Mohawk Ironworkers Build the City.* Bel Air, CA: Flash Point, 2010.

Wolny, Philip. *High-Risk Construction Work: Life Building Skyscrapers, Bridges, and Tunnels* (Extreme Careers). New York, NY: Rosen Publishing, 2009.

bibliography

American Society of Civil Engineers. "2013 Report Card for America's Infrastructure." Retrieved April 2015 (http://www.infrastructurereportcard.org).

Bello, Marisol. "Bridge Collapse Shines Light on Aging Infrastructure." *USA Today*, May 24, 2013. Retrieved April 2015 (http://www.usatoday.com/story/news/Nation/2013/05/24/washington-bridge-collapse-nations-bridges-deficient/2358419).

Berger, Joseph. "West Coast Weightlifter Arrives at Tappan Zee Site." *New York Times*, October 6, 2014. Retrieved March 2015 (http://www.nytimes.com/2014/10/07/Nyregion/giant-floating-crane-reaches-tappan-zee-site.html?_r=0).

Construction Equipment. "Mobile Inspection App Released." November 2, 2012. Retrieved April 2015 (http://www.constructionequipment.com/mobile-inspection-app-released).

De Laruelle, Scott. "Operating Toward a Bright Future: Heavy Equipment Instructors Talk Careers at Stoughton High School." *Stoughton Courier Hub*, November 10, 2013. Retrieved March 2015 (http://www.connectstoughton.com/articles/2013/11/10/operating-toward-bright-future).

GOARMY.com. "Horizontal Construction Engineer." Retrieved May 2015 (http://www.goarmy.com/careers-and-jobs/browse-career-and-job-categories/construction-engineering/construction-equipment-operator.html).

Grayson, Wayne. "Caterpillar's Predictive Diagnostics Will Enable More 'Repairs Before Failure' in Future Telematics Updates." *Equipment World*, March 12, 2015. Retrieved

May 2015 (http://www.equipmentworld.com/caterpillar-predictive-diagnostics-telematics).

Hagerty, James R. "Think You Can Drive A Bulldozer? Fearing Shortage of Skilled Operators, Machinery Makers Add Auto-Pilot Technologies." *Wall Street Journal*, August 26, 2013. Retrieved May 2015 (http://www.wsj.com/articles/SB100014241278873239806045790272616181888816).

Heavy Construction Academy. "Women Are Thriving in Heavy Equipment Work." January 19, 2012. Retrieved April 2015 (http://www.heavyconstructionacademy.com/2012/01/19/women-thriving-heavy-equipment/).

Hegewisch, Ariane, and Brigid O'Farrell. "Women in Construction and the Economic Recovery: Results from 2013 IWPR Tradeswomen Survey." Institute for Women's Policy Research, August 2014. Retrieved May 2015 (http://www.iwpr.org/publications/pubs/women-in-construction-and-the-economic-recovery-results-from-2013-iwpr-tradeswomen-survey).

International Union of Operating Engineers. "Heavy Equipment Operator (Operating Engineer)." Retrieved April 2015 (http://www.iuoe.org/jobs/heavy-equipment-operator).

Jackson, Tom. "Men vs. Women: Who Are the Better Heavy Equipment Operators?" *Equipment World*, July 31, 2014. Retrieved April 2015 (http://www.equipmentworld.com/men-vs-women-who-are-the-better-heavy-equipment-operators/).

Liming, Drew. "Careers in Green Construction." U.S. Bureau of Labor Statistics, June 2011. Retrieved May 2015 (http://www.bls.gov/green/construction/construction.pdf0).

Lubin, Gus, and Alexandra Mondalek. "The 16 Most Dangerous Jobs in America." *Business Insider*, August 5,

2013. Retrieved April 2015 (http://www.businessInsider.com/most-dangerous-jobs-in-america-2013-8#no-15-operating-engineers-and-construction-equipment-operators-2).

Maddox, Amanda. "Heavy Equipment Driving Topics." *Houston Chronicle*, May 7, 2013. Retrieved March 2015 (http://work.chron.com/heavy-equipment-driving-topics-28370.html).

Ryman, Richard. "Equipment Operators, Mechanics Needed for Timber Jobs." *Green Bay Press-Gazette*, December 4, 2014. Retrieved May 7, 2015 (http://www.greenbaypress-gazette.com/story/money/companies/state-of-opportunity/2014/11/10/equipment-operators-mechanics-needed-timber-industry/18816935).

Saeed, Khurram. "New Rochelle Crane Operator Takes Reins of Left Coast Lifter." *Journal News*, October 29, 2014. Retrieved May 2015 (http://www.lohud.com/Story/news/local/tappan-zee-bridge/2014/10/28/tz-crane-operator/18073087).

Service Canada. "Heavy Equipment Operators (Except Crane). Outlook." April 2013. Retrieved April 2015 (http://www.servicecanada.gc.ca/eng/qc/job_futures/statistics/7421.shtml).

Sinnema, Jodie. "Fast Career Tracks for Women." *Edmonton Journal*, January 7, 2014. Retrieved March 2015 (http://www.edmontonjournal.com/business/Fast+Career+tracks+women+with+video/9220976/story.html).

Smith, Greg B. "Dozens of Injuries at WTC Site Went Unreported." *New York Daily News*, November 3, 2014. Retrieved April 2015 (http://m.nydailynews.com/New-york/exclusive-dozens-injuries-wtc-site-unreported-article-1.1996945).

U.S. Bureau of Labor Statistics. "Construction Equipment Operators. Occupational Outlook Handbook." Retrieved

May 2015 (http://www.bls.gov.oog/construction-and-extraction/mobile/construction-equipment-operators.htm).

U.S. Bureau of Labor Statistics. "Employed Persons by Detailed Occupation. Occupational Outlook Handbook." Retrieved May 2015 (http://www.bls.gov/cps/cpsaat11.pdf).

Wake Tech Community College. "Wake Tech to Train Heavy Equipment Operators with High-Tech Tools." October 29, 2014. Retrieved April 2015 (http://www.waketech.edu/news/ake-tech-train-heavy-equipment-operators-high-tech-tools#.VVj5YaaH87A).

index

S

T

U

W

About the Author

Henrietta Toth is a writer and editor with nearly twenty years' experience in academic publishing. She has become interested in heavy equipment while watching the construction of the New NY Bridge from her own backyard.

Photo Credits

Cover, p. 1 (figure) michaeljung/Shutterstock.com; cover, p. 1 (background) Girodjl/Shutterstock.com; p. 4 © iStockphoto.com/lutherhill; p. 8 Vadim Ratnikov/Shutterstock.com; p. 10 NARA/National Archives at Denver; pp. 12-13 cdrin/Shutterstock.com; p. 14 China Photos/Getty Images; p. 17 TTstudio/Shutterstock.com; pp. 18-19 AFP/Getty Images; p. 21 Arina P Habich/Shutterstock.com; pp. 24-25, 56-57 © AP Images; p. 27 TFoxFoto/Shutterstock.com; pp. 28-29 Pacific Press/LightRocket/Getty Images; pp. 33, 40-41 U.S. Army photo by Staff Sgt. Debralee Best; pp. 34-35 US Department of Labor/flickr; pp. 36-37 © iStockphoto.com/Chris Schmidt; pp. 42-43 © iStockphoto.com/stocknroll; pp. 46-47 Chip Somodevilla/Getty Images; p. 51 Business Wire/Getty Images; pp. 52-53 Joe Amon/The Denver Post/Getty Images; pp. 60-61 Robert Nickelsberg/Hulton Archive/Getty Images; pp. 64-65 Elmer Martinez/AFP/Getty Images

Designer: Matt Cauli; Editor: Meredith Day; Photo Researcher: Nicole DiMella